# DIVERSITY STRATEGIC PLANNING REPORT:
# AN ENVIRONMENTAL SCAN OF
# U.S. THEOLOGICAL SCHOOLS

Jessica Davis, M.Div., J.D., D.Min.

ISBN: 0615998194
ISBN-13: 978-0615998190

Faith & Public Policy Institute Inc.
www.faithpolicyinstitute.org

Princeton, N.J.      Washington, D.C.

# DEDICATION

Faith & Public Policy Institute Inc.

# CONTENTS

# ACKNOWLEDGMENTS

Faith Policy Staff
ATS staff

# CHAPTER I
## INTRODUCTION

Introduction

The Association of Theological Schools (ATS), founded in 1918, is a North American membership organization of more than 250 Protestant, Roman Catholic, and Orthodox graduate schools in the United States and Canada that grant post-baccalaureate professional and academic degrees. These schools represent a broad spectrum of doctrinal, ecclesiastical, and theological perspectives. These ATS schools educate persons for ecclesiastical leadership and for teaching and research in the theological disciplines. The mission of ATS is to promote the improvement and enhancement of theological education in the United States and Canada. ATS seeks to fulfill this mission through a commitment to diversity, quality and improvement, collegiality, and leadership. The ATS Commission on Accrediting, recognized by the U.S. Department of Education and Council for Higher Education Accreditation, accredits these theological schools and approves degree programs offered by these accredited schools (ATS, 2011).

The Association of Theological Schools is the context for this qualitative research study. The goal of this study is to conduct an environmental scan of the strategic racial and ethnic minority plans being implemented at the accredited ATS schools in the

United States affiliated with the largest mainstream Protestant denominations in the United States which identified and responded to the opportunities and threats impacting racial and ethnic minority administrators, faculty, staff, and students and their institutional climates. The goal of this environmental scan is to assist the Association of Theological Schools and its mainstream Protestant schools with understanding, anticipating, and responding to the threats and opportunities in the changing external environment that ATS and its schools have already begun to identify statistically in their annual surveys (Morrison, 1992). More specifically, the purpose of this study is to assist the Association of Theological Schools in fulfilling its mission to assist its accredited U.S. theological schools with effectively responding to the changing ethnic and racial demographics taking place in the United States and as a result at their schools and churches by providing ATS with a comparative assessment of the most recent strategic minority plans of its mainstream Protestant ATS schools. This qualitative research study provides a comparison of the most recent strategic minority plans on identifying and responding to the opportunities and threats impacting racial and ethnic minority administrators, faculty, staff, and students and their institutional climates at the mainstream Protestant ATS schools in the United States.

The next section of this research study report provides the research problem for this qualitative research study, "An Environmental Scan of Racial and Ethnic Minority Strategic Planning at U.S. Accredited Theological Schools."

## Statement of the Problem

The Executive Director, Dr. Daniel Aleshire, of The Association of Theological Schools states, "ATS schools have not been asleep at the switch, but the world around them has changed faster and perhaps more pervasively than the schools have. Schools have adapted practices and modified structures, but ultimately, realities beyond the schools will require even more fundamental shifts in institutional form and educational character (Aleshire, 2010, p. 4)." The racial and ethnic minority administrators, staff, faculty, and student demographics at ATS schools do not reflect the racial and ethnic demographics of the United States (Cascante-Gomez, 2008, 21). "In North America, theological education-still dominated by white male,

Euro-centric perspectives that unconsciously, and sometimes consciously-mirrors in different degrees the still prevalent racism of the broader culture (Cascante-Gomez, 2008, 22)."

According to the "Diversity in Theological Education (ATS, 2011)" and "The Future has Arrived: Changing Theological Education in a Changing World (Aleshire, 2010)," the growth in total enrollment is in large part due to the increase in racial and ethnic minority students since 1990 while majority students' enrollment has declined or remained static at many of the graduate schools. The racial and ethnic enrollment at theological schools has grown from less than 3% in 1969 to approximately 24% in 2010 (ATS, 2011 and Aleshire, 2010). The faculty of color has changed as well according to ATS (Aleshire, 2010). The percentage of faculty of color has grown from 8% in 1990 to 15% in 2010 (Aleshire, 2010, p.4). Dr. Aleshire states: "Changes in the composition of the faculties and student bodies reflect the changing composition of the population and the shifting roles in religious leadership (Aleshire, 2010, p.4)."

While enrollment is increasing, it is far from being representative of the percentage of racial and ethnic minorities in the U.S. population (Davis, Hernandez & Wilson, 2002, p. 72). According to the U.S. Census Bureau (2001), Asians are approximately 3% of the population, Blacks or African Americans are 12% of the population, Hispanics or Latinos are 12% of the population and Whites are 72% of the population. The director of student information resources at ATS, Frances A. Lonsway, states: "…the seminaries of ATS enroll a higher proportion of

Asians than are present in the population, a lower proportion of Blacks, and considerably lower proportion of Hispanics-the most underrepresented racial/ethnic group in theological education (Lonsway, 2002, p.52)." According to Davis, Hernandez, and Wilson (2002), the growth that we actually see in racial and ethnic minority students and faculty at ATS schools is a reflection of new schools being added to membership in the Association.

The next section of this report describes why this study on racial and ethnic minority strategic planning at U.S. accredited theological schools is important to research.

## Significance of the Study

The relevancy of theological education in the United States in the 21$^{st}$ century will depend on the ability of the theological schools to adapt to changes in the external environments that impact their organizations and affect their ability to accomplish the mission of educating persons for ecclesiastical leadership and for teaching and research in the theological disciplines (ATS, 2011; Morrison, 1985; Morrison, 1992; Speller, 2002). Dr. Fernando Cascante-Gomez, assistant professor of Christian education at Union Theological Seminary and Presbyterian School of Christian Education in New York, states that the challenges of racial and ethnic diversity in theological education will become more urgent because of the growing demands of the changing sociocultural realities in the United States (Cascante-Gomez, 2008, p. 35). "Despite efforts to increase racial and ethnic diversity in theological education during the last three decades, some but not enough progress has been made (Cascante-Gomez, 2008, 21)."

The underrepresentation of these racial and ethnic minority groups in theological education has adversely impacted theological and religious studies and the communities that these groups represent according to Mejido (1998). Specifically, the underrepresentation has impacted the course offerings and curricula (Mejido, 1998, p.64). "One student expressed this fact thus: 'I have taken classes from professors who don't integrate any cross-cultural concern in their courses; the history of the church is the history of the European church and that's all....

They never talk to you about your culture or if they do, they just do it in one day or half an hour.'" The underrepresentation has created a monolithic and ethnocentric education and as a result, students have been robbed of opportunities to be exposed to the diversity of religious experiences in the U.S. according to Mejido (1998).

Theological schools are now being confronted in more profound ways with the realities of a growing pluralism in the United States according to Speller (2002), an African American church historian and religious educator. Speller (2002) states that if our mission is to prepare women and men for effective ecclesiastical leadership, we will fall short of the mission with a theological education that does not reflect the realities of the diversity in our communities. As a result of these new realities, institutions are being forced to review their tradition of an exclusive curriculum, a homogenous faculty, and a static or declining majority student population (Speller, 2002). In light of these significant demographic changes, the diversification of the administrators, faculty, staff, and students along with changes in policies and practices become essential parts of the future relevance of theological institutions in the United States (Speller, 2002). ATS schools have a responsibility to provide racial and ethnic minority students with faculty, mentors and conversation partners from their own racial and ethnic groups (Mejido, 1998). This responsibility must be a priority in their strategic planning as they assess the recruitment, retention, and graduation rates of their racial and ethnic minority students.

The next section of this report provides the guiding research questions for this qualitative research study on racial and ethnic minority strategic planning at the mainstream Protestant U.S. accredited theological schools.

## Research Questions

The research questions are designed to help me understand whether the mainstream Protestant accredited theological schools in the United States have identified the threats and opportunities impacting their racial and ethnic minority administrators, faculty, staff, and students and institutional climate. Then once I identify whether these schools have identified the threats and opportunities, I want to know whether these ATS schools have prioritized a response to the threats and opportunities in their strategic planning. The following are the guiding research questions for this qualitative research study.

1. How many of the accredited mainstream Protestant ATS schools in the United States have implemented strategic minority plans in order to respond to the threats and opportunities impacting their racial and ethnic minority administrators, faculty, staff, and students and their institutional climates as identified by the Association of Theological Schools?

2. How are the mainstream Protestant ATS schools in the United States responding to and preparing for the threats and opportunities in the changing external environment impacting

their racial and ethnic minority administrators, faculty, staff, and students and institutional climate as identified in their strategic plans?

3.  Do the mainstream Protestant ATS schools in the United States have a shared understanding in their strategic minority planning of high priority issues in the changing environmental threats and opportunities impacting their racial and ethnic minority administrators, faculty, staff, and students and their institutional climates?

The next section of this report provides the intended use of the results and conclusions for this qualitative research study.

## Purpose of the Study

One of the goals of the Association of Theological Schools is to promote awareness of the diversity of race and ethnicity widely present in North America in order for theological schools to remain relevant in our changing cultural and racially diverse communities (Speller, 2002). Specifically, the ATS General Institutional Standard states, "Schools shall seek to enhance participation of persons of racial/ethnic minorities in institutional life (ATS, 2002, p. 50)." The purpose of this qualitative research study is to provide the Association of Theological Schools with a mainstream Protestant denominational assessment of the most recent strategic minority plans of approximately 19% of the ATS accredited theological schools in the United States in order to assist the Association with fulfilling its diversity mission to assist their accredited schools with effectively identifying and responding to the changing ethnic and racial demographics taking place in the United States and as a result at its theological schools in order to ensure continued theological relevance in their changing communities.

The next chapter of this report provides the literature review for this qualitative research study. The literature review includes primary and secondary sources on environmental scanning, strategic planning in higher education, critical pedagogy, critical race theory, and minorities in higher education. Each area of review has informed the development of my research study, "An Environmental Scan of Racial and Ethnic Minority Strategic Planning at U.S. Accredited Theological Schools."

# CHAPTER 2
## LITERATURE REVIEW

### Introduction

The literature review contextualizes the research questions in the study which provides the reader with what he or she needs to know in order to understand the significance of this study (Foss & Waters, 2007, pg.53). This literature review includes primary and secondary sources on environmental scanning, strategic planning in higher education, critical pedagogy, critical race theory, and the state of racial and ethnic minorities in higher education. Each area of review has informed the development of the framework of this qualitative research study, "An Environmental Scan of Racial and Ethnic Minority Strategic Planning at U.S. Accredited Theological Schools."

The next section of this chapter provides the review of literature on environmental scanning and reveals how it has informed the development of this qualitative research study. Environmental scanning is a method began by major corporations to understand the external environment of their organizations for the purpose of strategic planning. As a result of its origin, environmental scanning is a relatively new method in theological strategic planning in higher education so very little is presently written. However, I have identified the most relevant environmental scanning periodicals in the next section for this qualitative research study.

## Environmental Scanning

The traditional long-range planning models with focus primarily on internal analyses that include the organization's vision, mission, strengths and weaknesses versus external analyses that include understanding the organization's changing external environment do not allow institutions to anticipate environmental changes with enough advance time to make the needed institutional changes in order to respond effectively to approaching shifts in the environment that impact the organization (Cope, 1981 and Morrison, 1992). Environmental scanning initially used by major corporations and trade and professional associations but now being used by colleges and universities is a method that enables institutions to understand the external environment and to translate this understanding into strategic planning processes (Morrison, 1992 and Morrison, Renfro & Boucher, 1983).

Environmental scanning is the systematic collection of information from both external and internal sources in order to provide early warnings to the institution of changing external conditions that impact the organization (Aguilar, 1967 and Morrison, 1992). These systematic collections include external information from economic, political, social, and technological developments (Morrison, Renfro & Boucher, 1983). Major state, regional, and national periodicals constitute significant external scanning resources for these developments (Morrison, 1985). These systematic collections also include internal information form administrators and faculty. "Key administrators and faculty members can be interviewed to identify emerging issues that they believe may affect the institution in the future and that are not now receiving the attention they will eventually merit." (Morrison, 1985, pg. 32).

The goal of environmental scanning is to help the institution identify potentially significant external changes with enough lead time to react to the changes (Morrison, 1992). The objectives of an environmental scan include identifying trends that are important to the institution; defining the potential threats, opportunities, or changes implied by the trends; and alerting the institution to trends that are converging, diverging, speeding up, slowing down, or interacting (Coates, 1985 and Morrison, 1992). An effective environmental scan assists with the strategic direction of the institution by enabling the institution to understand current and potential changes in its external environment (Fahey & Naravanan, 1986 and Morrison, 1992).

The next section of this chapter provides the review of literature on strategic planning in higher education and reveals how it has informed the development of this qualitative research study. The central tenet of strategic planning in higher education is to align the institution of higher education with its external environment (Rowley, D.J., Lujan, H.D. & Dolence, M.G., 1997,   pg. 53).

## Strategic Planning

"Strategic planning is a formal process designed to help an organization identify and maintain an optimal alignment with the most important elements of its environment (Rowley, D.J., Lujan, H.D. & Dolence, M.G., 1997, pg. 15)." Strategic planning has been a respectful method for purposeful change in the private sectors for decades (Rowley, D.J., Lujan, H.D. & Dolence, M.G., 1997, pg. vi). However, when higher education institutions began to use this method in the late 1970s and 1980s the results were mix (Rowley, D.J., Lujan, H.D. & Dolence, M.G., 1997, pg. 8). These mixed results were unfortunate because the organizations that engaged strategic planning demonstrated benefits over the organizations that did not (Rowley, D.J., Lujan, H.D. & Dolence, M.G., 1997, pg. 8). The early mix results have not prevented this method of assessment from making its impact on higher education.

Strategic planning is the most common tool used by higher education institutions today to identify and respond to their external environments (Dalrympie, M., 2009, pg. 4). The ability to align the higher education institution with its environment is one of the strengths of strategic planning (Dalrympie, M., 2009, pg. 4). "If strategic leadership is to respond effectively to change, it needs a set of disciplinary tools… It has to find appropriate ways to grasp the realities of change in the wider world. In the standard practices of strategic planning, this is called an environmental scan (Morrill, 2007, pg. 156)." Environmental scanning is a growing method being utilized in strategic planning in higher education, because of what is now being asked of the external environment facilitated by the institutions' stakeholders.

The end of the twentieth century marks the beginning of the end of the academy operating independently from the external environment (Rowley, D.J., Lujan, H.D. & Dolence, M.G., 1997, pg. 16). Higher education in the United States began primarily as private schools founded and funded by religious institutions (Rowley, D.J., Lujan, H.D. & Dolence, M.G., 1997, pg. 16). The public universities that were established through federal land grants authorized by the Morrill Act of 1862 emulated the private schools' insularity (Rowley, D.J., Lujan, H.D. & Dolence, M.G., 1997, pg. 17). "The combinations of sectarian origins, medieval traditions, dedication to free speech, and job security derived from tenure have preserved the academy from unwanted and injurious intrusion (Rowley, D.J., Lujan, H.D. & Dolence, M.G., 1997, pg. 17)." This autonomy has been allowed to flourish for centuries until the restructuring of the economy and the growing need for additional taxes to support higher education in the late twentieth century (Rowley, D.J., Lujan, H.D. & Dolence, M.G., 1997, pg. 17). Higher education is now being challenged to realign their insularity to fit this new age (Rowley, D.J., Lujan, H.D. & Dolence, M.G., 1997, pg. 18). "While strategic planning can be a tool in a number of ways for achieving this transition, its central contribution is to align the institution with opportunities and constraints in its environment (Rowley, D.J., Lujan, H.D. & Dolence, M.G., 1997, pg. 52)."

Finally, in addition to strategic planning's strength of environmental alignment, strategic planning also provides an important process benefit. One of the process benefits is the impact on the institutional culture or climate (Dalrympie, M., 2009, pg. 5). According to Morrill (2007), one of the central themes in strategic planning in higher education is that the higher education institution functions as a culture (norms and beliefs, customs and rituals, and stories and traditions) as well as a formal organization (Morrill, 2007, pg. 222). The implementation phase of a strategic plan requires knowing the "folkways, pathways and leverage points" within the culture of the organization to get things done (Morrill, 2007, pg. 222).

In conclusion, the growing use of strategic planning in higher education reveals that changes usually come from a major crisis, outside pressure or a farsighted leader (Rowley, D.J., Lujan, H.D. & Dolence, M.G., 1997, pg. 9). Whether strategic planning comes out of crisis, pressure, or vision, strategic planning requires prioritizing the use of the institution's resources to the benefit of the present and future of the institution (Rowley, D.J., Lujan, H.D. & Dolence, M.G., 1997, pg. 9). The assessment of a strategic plan and the results of a strategic plan can inform the next round of strategic planning and the setting of future priorities (Dalrympie, M., 2009, pg. 5).

The next section of this chapter provides the review of literature on Critical Pedagogy and Critical Race Theory. This section reveals how Critical Pedagogy and Critical Race Theory have informed the theoretical development of this qualitative research study. Critical Pedagogy has been defined as Critical Race Theory within education (Darder, A., Baltodano, M. & Torres, R., 2003).

Critical Pedagogy

The theoretical framework for this qualitative research study has been informed by Critical Pedagogy and Critical Race Theory. According to *The Critical Pedagogy Reader* (2003), Critical Race Theory (CRT) within education is a critical pedagogy. In other words, CRT in education is a theoretical lens that requires a critical thinker (Darder, A., Baltodano, M. & Torres, R., 2003).

CRT is a social justice movement launched by Derrick Bell and Alan Freeman and other law scholars of color in the 1970s to challenge how race and racial power were constructed in American Society (Crenshaw, Gotanda, Peller, & Thomas, 1995; Delgado & Stefancic, 2000; Delgado & Stefancic, 2001). They believed that the Civil Rights

Movement of the 1960s had stopped and that many of its gains were being rolled back so they began a critique of the constructs of race and racism in American society in order to prepare for social change (Delgado & Stefancic, 2000, pg. xvi). These critical race theorists believe race and racism function as central pillars of hegemonic power in American culture (Crenshaw, Gotanda, Peller, & Thomas, 1995, pg. xxii). "Hegemony refers to a process of social control that is carried out through the moral and intellectual leadership of a dominant social culture class over subordinate groups (Darder, A., Baltodano, M. & Torres, R., 2003, pg. 13)." Therefore, CRT locates itself in the intersection of critical theory and racism and the law (Crenshaw, Gotanda, Peller, & Thomas, 1995, pg. xxvi).

CRT provides a theoretical framework for a contemporary movement that examines the relationship among race, racism and power. The main interest of the CRT movement is to understand how white supremacy and its subordination of people of color has been created and maintained in American culture. The movement does not just want to understand the roles of race, racism, and power, but the advocates of CRT want to change it for the better. (Crenshaw, Gotanda, Peller, & Thomas, 1995; Delgado & Stefancic, 2000; Delgado & Stefancic, 2001).

The advocates of CRT argue that racism is not aberrational in our culture but has become an ordinary part of the everyday experience of most people of color. This ordinary part of everyday life has served both the psychic and material purposes of white elites, materially, and working class, physically, according to CRT. As a result of racism benefiting these two segments of the population, Delgado and Stefancic argued that a large segment of the population does not have any incentives in eradicating racism in American culture. (Crenshaw, Gotanda, Peller, & Thomas, 1995; Delgado & Stefancic, 2000; Delgado & Stefancic, 2001).

The next major theme discussed within the CRT movement is that race is a social construction. According to CRT, race is not objective, inherent, or fixed. According to Delgado and Stefancic (2001), races are categories that society invents, manipulates, and or retires when convenient. If this is true and it is, the roles of race, racism, and power in American culture can be changed for the better.

Critical race theorists have a significant role in empowering the American citizenry in understanding that race is a social construct and can be changed in a way that does not just benefit one particular group. This type of systemic change requires critical thinking with an awareness of the roles of race, racism, and power in American culture. This contemporary theoretical framework, Critical Race Theory, becomes a critical pedagogy within education (Darder, Baltodano & Torres, 2003; Delgado & Stefancic, 2001; Freire, 1998; Freire, 1993; Hincey, 2004; Kumashiro, 2004; Santrock, 2001).

The critical pedagogical perspective is to empower the culturally marginalized and economically disenfranchised student (Darder, A., Baltodano, M. & Torres, R., 2003, pg. 11). "From the standpoint of economics, public schools served the position of select groups within an asymmetrical power relations that serve to replicate the existing values and privileges of the culture of the dominate class (Darder, A., Baltodano, M. & Torres, R., 2003, pg. 11)." Critical Pedagogy challenges the class reproduction taking place at schools as a result of the daily social practices that perpetuate racialized inequalities (Darder, A., Baltodano, M. & Torres, R., 2003, pg. 11). "It is these uncontested relationships between schools and society that Critical Pedagogy seeks to challenge, unmasking traditional claims that education provides equal opportunity and access to all (Darder, A., Baltodano, M. & Torres, R., 2003, pg. 11)."

Critical Pedagogy challenges educators to critique and transform hegemonic practices in their classrooms (Darder, A., Baltodano, M. & Torres, R.,

2003, pg. 13). Kumashiro (2004) describes this critique and transformation as "anti-oppressive education." An anti-oppressive education has three major approaches according to Kumashiro (2004). The first approach is to improve the experiences of the marginalized and disadvantaged students in the classroom (Kumashiro, K., 2004, pg. xxv). Secondly, an anti-oppressive education challenges and changes the knowledge that all students have about people who have been identified as different (Kumashiro, K., 2004, pg. xxv). The third approach is to focus on identifying and challenging the dynamics in society that privilege one group and disadvantage another (Kumashiro, K., 2004, pg. xxv). Collectively, these three approaches provide an educational environment for the development of a critical social consciousness by the student as well as the educator (Darder, A.,

Baltodano, M. & Torres, R., 2003, pg. 15). This critical social consciousness is an "awareness of the social realities that shape their lives and discover their own capacities to recreate them (Darder, A., Baltodano, M. & Torres, R., 2003, pg. 15).

In conclusion, an anti-oppressive education informed by Critical Pedagogy challenges educators to become critical thinkers  in order to understand how their life experiences have shaped their thinking as well as that of their students for the purpose of being empowered to dismantle racism in American society one classroom at a time (Hinchey, P.H., 2004, pg. 44).

The next section of this chapter provides the review of literature on racial and ethnic minorities in higher education and how it has informed the development of this qualitative research study. A predominately white higher education institution that is operating in the United States without a critical pedagogy will not be able to effectively identify the barriers in the development of racial and ethnic minority students.

## Minorities in Higher Education

In the context of Critical Pedagogy, predominately white higher education institutions are failing to facilitate the critical learning and development of their racial and ethnic minority students. Therefore, they are failing to facilitate the critical learning of all their students. A predominately white higher education institution that is operating in the United States without a critical pedagogy will not be able to effectively identify the barriers in the development of racial and ethnic minority students as revealed in part in the declining enrollment, retention, and graduation rates of racial and ethnic minority students during the last 40 years. These predominately white institutions' inability to create an effective student development model for racial and ethnic minority students has been reproduced across the nation as revealed in the national enrollment, retention, and graduation challenges of racial and ethnic students. How do "critical educators" begin to disrupt the "social reproduction" of an ineffective student development model for racial and ethnic minority students in higher education? In order to answer this question, I examined the social practices that are presently being reproduced at predominately white higher education institutions in the United States. (Hinchey, 2004 & Tsui, 2003).

What is the reality today for racial and ethnic minority students? The reality is disturbing as we see the enrollment numbers decline which has and will impact graduate and professional schools. In the 1960s and 1970s, the enrollment numbers of racial and ethnic minority students were steadily increasing, and retention rates were gaining strength. Then something happened in the 1980s. The enrollment and retentions rates began to decline and the rates are still declining today (Kobrak, 1992, p.509). What happened?

The Commission on Minority Participation and Education in America states, "America is moving backward not forward with its efforts to achieve the full participation of minority citizens in the life of prosperity of the nation (Kobrak, 1992, p. 509)." This statement is the backdrop for the concept of social reproduction. What are higher education institutions reproducing? In response to this question, the Commission is stating that higher education student development policy as it is today is not acting in the best interest of the racial and ethnic minority student (Kobrak, 1992, p. 509).

How do we begin to turn these declining enrollment, retention, and graduation numbers around for the racial and ethnic minority student? One of the core issues is the worldview of the racial and ethnic minority student in contrast to the worldview of the institution of higher education. The worldview is the distinct way people get through reality. The worldview includes their guiding beliefs of basic assumptions about life. It gives culture its identity and distinctiveness. However, there are multiple worldviews. The predominately white higher education institutions facilitate the development and learning of their students as if there is only one worldview. This lack of diversity in worldviews is at the core of the decline of enrollment, retention, and graduation rates of racial and ethnic minority students in education in the United States today (Johnson, 2003, p. 820).

What are the differences between the racial and ethnic minority student's worldview and the white majority student's worldview? The guiding principles of the white student's worldview are control over nature and survival of the fittest. This control and survival worldview is decided with competition, individual rights, independence and separateness. The guiding principles of the racial and ethnic minority student can be characterized as being one with nature in survival of the people. This worldview emphasizes cooperation, dependence, and collective responsibility. Collective responsibility is significant in understanding the types of teaching approaches needed to facilitate critical student learning and development. Many racial and ethnic minority students are struggling in the present competitive and individualistic environments of many of our institutions of higher education. Minority students would improve in their learning and development if these institutions of higher education would incorporate a more cooperative teaching methodology, taking in consideration the diversity of worldviews (Johnson, 2003, p. 821).

The perceptions and self-perceptions of minority students also have significant influences on the learning and development of racial and ethnic minority students. These perceptions include educational expectations. Why are expectations important? Educational expectations have a direct effect on school and student outcomes (Cheng, 2002, p. 306). Minority students at predominately white institutions have perceived their schools as hostile places. Minority students often see their relationships with white professors and students as demoralizing (Kobrak, 1992, p. 518).

White students who hold negative stereotypes and attitudes towards minority students hinder minority student adjustment and persistence at the institution of higher education. These stereotypes create a culture of hostility at these predominately white institutions. Incidents of discriminations created by faculty or fed by faculty have increased from 34% in 1988 to 43% in 1996 (Suarez-Balcazar, Orellana-Damacela, Portillo, Rowan & Andrews-

Guillen, July/August 2003, p. 430). If there is a perception that the student's school environment is a hostile place and this same student does not have a positive relationship with his or her professors, it becomes clear why enrollment and retention challenges have increased over the last 30 years. Positive interaction between the student and professor is key to a student's success. In order to understand the power of perception and expectation, the next section will do a minority comparison with Asian-American students. Asian Americans have been described as the "model minority" group (Kobrak, 1992, p. 519).

Since the 1960s, Asian Americans have been portrayed by the press and media as the successful minority group (Wong, Chienping Faith Lai, Nagasawa & Lin, 1998, p. 96). This image has made both a positive and negative social and psychological impact on the lives of Asian-American students. Some Asian-American students struggle as much as their African-American colleagues at these predominately white institutions of higher education, but they don't feel comfortable articulating their struggles given the stereotypes they live under as part of this model minority group. Many live under greater levels of stress than other minority students as a result of being the recipients of this 50 year perception. As a result of this perception, educators have ignored the real performances of Asian-American students and continue to believe the images promoted by the media (Wong, Chienping Faith Lai, Nagasawa & Lin, 1998, p. 97). These media promoted images of Asian- Americans is not entirely reality. Southeast Asian-Americans and Pacific

Islanders who are poorly educated and underemployed are not taken into consideration (Wong, Chienping Faith Lai, Nagasawa & Lin, 1998a, p. 100).

The perception of academic excellence has made the following impact on Asian Americans: studying longer hours, taking fewer classes, enduring loneliness and isolation, and restricting their career choices. This student population has been impacted negatively in many ways and there is rarely a public discussion in academia about it. Predominately white institutions assume Asian-American students are okay. Are Asian-American students the model minority (Wong, Chienping Faith Lai, Nagasawa & Lin, 1998, p. 98)?

What is the difference between the Asian-American student and the African-American student?

African-American students have equal or higher self-esteem in academic self-concepts in comparison to white students (Schmader, Major & Gramzow, 2002, p. 118). African-American students value academic success highly and sometimes more highly than white students (Schmader, Major & Gramzow, 2002, p. 118). The difference between the Asian-American student and the African-American student is the fact that the perceptions and expectations are negative in different but parallel ways. These negative perceptions cause the African-American student to disengage from the academic community in order to survive in an environment that has become a threat because of the levels of hostility being experienced by the student daily. The African-American student is expected to thrive in an environment that does not celebrate or recognize his or her worldview. In addition to the lack of recognition for the student's belief system as a viable system of thought, the student is dealing with issues of discrimination, negative perceptions from their colleagues and faculty. The student is not able to connect with classmates or faculty so he or she disengages to survive. Many African-American students disengage their feelings or self-worth from the academic outcomes as part of their survival mechanism. They disengage from the academic community to escape the anxiety that results from performing under the weight of the stereotypes of inferiority. This survival response is called "psychological disengagement" (Schmader, Major & Gramzow, 2002, p. 116).

As a result of this psychological disengagement, test scores and grades no longer become a motivator to achieve academic success.

Psychological disengagement is another reason for the growing enrollment, retention, and graduation challenges being experienced by racial and ethnic minority students in white institutions of higher education across the nation. Psychological disengagement is the final reason identified in this literature review for the growing enrollment, retention, and graduation challenges of many minority students (Schmader, Major & Gramzow, 2002, p. 116).

The next chapter of this report provides the research methodology, the case study method, for this qualitative research study. Multisite case studies are comparative cases studies. This qualitative research study will conduct multisite case studies of the mainstream Protestant denominations and their affiliated theological graduate schools.

# CHAPTER 3
## METHODOLOGY

## Rationale of Research Design

This qualitative research study, "An Environmental Scan of Racial and Ethnic Minority Strategic Planning at U.S. Accredited Theological Schools" is an environmental scan of the strategic racial and ethnic minority plans being implemented at accredited ATS schools in the United States that are affiliated with mainstream Protestant denominations and have begun to identify and respond to the opportunities and threats impacting racial and ethnic minority administrators, faculty, staff, and students and their institutional climates as documented by the Association of Theological Schools. The purpose of this qualitative research study is to provide the Association of Theological Schools with a mainstream Protestant denominational assessment of the most recent strategic minority plans of the ATS accredited theological schools in the United States in order to assist the Association with fulfilling its diversity mission.

The mainstream Protestant denominations in the United States are reportedly in crisis (Frank, pg. 21). "There is a startling difference between viewing recent church history through a paradigm of illness, decline, and fragmentation, and seeing it as a story of an emerging church encompassing many cultural ways and becoming a global communion (Frank, pg.

31)." Frank (2006) states that the five largest Protestant denominations reported their highest membership totals in the 1960s. However, by the end of the 1980s and 1990s, the United Methodists reported losses of approximately 25% of their membership, the Episcopalians loss almost 30%, the Presbyterians loss almost 30%, and the Disciples astonishingly loss almost 50% (Frank, pg. 25). According to Frank (2006), we must look beyond the actual numbers to understand the reason for the numerical decline of these mainstream Protestant denominations since the 1960s. "There are a number of demographic and sociological factors that more clearly account for the numbers, help to reinterpret the past, and point toward the contours of the emerging church (Frank, pg. 27)." Many of these mainstream Protestant churches are located in communities of major population loss or shift (Frank, pg. 28). "Some rural counties have lost three-fourth of their population in fifteen years. The megachurches of the 1920s, built on prime sites along trolley lines in city neighborhoods and accommodating huge auditoriums, gymnasiums, and even bowling alleys, have seen their members migrate to the suburbs (Frank, pg. 28)." According to Frank (2006), these population shifts during the last forty years have made the United States a dislocated society. "These shifts, combines with the startling estimate that over one-fourth of the U.S. population changes residence in any given year, mark a severely dislocated society. Many residents of any metropolitan area are not natives and view themselves as transient (Frank, pg.28)." As a result, many churches are hosting first and second generation immigrants from Korea, the

Pacific Islands, Central America, the Philippines, the Caribbean, and sub-Saharan Africa (Frank, pg. 32). "As the U.S. continues to add significantly more Hispanic, Asian, and other people to its predominate population of European and African heritage , the churches will be challenged to respond by founding even more diverse congregations and raising up leaders from within various ethnic groups (Frank, pg. 32)."

The present state of affairs of mainstream Protestant denominations leads to the reason for the design of this qualitative research study and the core question, "How are the mainstream Protestant accredited schools responding to and preparing for the threats and opportunities in the racial and ethnic shift taking place in the United States today as they recruit diverse students from these communities of faith, prepare diverse ecclesiastical leadership, and retain their relevance in a shifting racially and ethnically diverse society?" This qualitative research study used the case study method to answer this core research question along with the guiding research questions identified in this report.

The denominations and their theological schools have a symbiotic relationship. Therefore, this relationship provides a useful way to organize the research. The research is organized according to denominational affiliations utilizing the case study approach. The next section of this chapter will discuss the type of case study method utilized for this qualitative research study.

## Research Design

This qualitative research study is a study on strategic racial and ethnic planning presently being conducted at accredited ATS schools in the United States utilizing the multisite case study method. (Foss & Waters, 2007; Merriam, 2009; Yin, 2009). "Qualitative case studies share with other forms of qualitative research the search for meaning and understanding, the researcher as the primary instrument of data collection and analysis, an inductive investigative strategy, and the end product being richly descriptive (Merriam, 2009, p.39). Multisite case studies are commonly referred to as collective case studies or comparative case studies (Merriam, 2009, P. 49). Collective cases are usually categorically bound together because they are members of the same group (Merriam, 2009, p.49). In this qualitative research study, the accredited mainstream Protestant ATS schools in the United States will be categorized according to their denominational affiliations. Dr. Sharan Merriam, professor of adult education at the University of Georgia, states that the more cases in your research study makes the interpretation more compelling and enhances the reliability, validity and generalizability of the findings (Merriam, 2009, pg. 50).

However, the strength of utilizing multisite case studies is also its challenge because it is arduous to manage and analyze multiple cases (Merriam, 2009, p. 50). The other challenges with utilizing the case study method are the limitations that come with the researcher because "the researcher is the primary instrument of data collection and analysis (Merriam,

2009, p.52)." According to Robert Stake, the author of "Qualitative Case Studies," the researcher must decide how to make the study a story, decide how much to compare cases with other cases, decide whether to formulize generalizations, and decide how much to protect the anonymity of the respondents (Stake, 2005, p. 460). Therefore the researcher must be aware of biases that she brings to the final product of the research study (Merriam, 2009, p. 52).

The researcher of the study recognize that her experiences as an African American administrator at predominately white higher education institutions have informed and biased my research. "The strength of qualitative approaches is that they account for and include difference-ideologically, epistemologically, methodologically –and most importantly, humanly. They do not attempt to eliminate what cannot be discounted. They do not attempt to simplify what cannot be simplified. Thus, it is precisely because case study includes paradoxes and acknowledges that there are no simple answers, which it can and should qualify as the gold standard (Shield, 2007, p.13)."

The next section of this methodology chapter provides the sampling method chosen for this case study approach with the assistance of research and programmatic staff from the Association of Theological Schools.

## Sampling Method

The case study approach requires nonprobabilistic or purposeful sampling (Merriam, 2009, p. 77). "Purposeful sampling is based on the assumption that the investigator wants to discover, understand, and gain insight and therefore must select a sample from which the most can be learn (Merriam, 2009, p.77)." In consultation with the ATS director of student information and organizational evaluation and ATS director of leadership education, I identified a sample of accredited ATS schools in the United States that I used for this research study. Each school has a representative, president or dean of the theological school, in the sample. Two levels of sampling are used with qualitative case studies (Merriam, 2009, p. 81). The survey was sent to the identified representatives in the sample developed in consultation with the ATS staff, but the analysis will be done with the second level of the sampling, the actual respondents which usually represent a percentage of the initial sample. In consultation with the ATS director of leadership education and the results of the pilot study conducted, I developed an online questionnaire utilizing an online survey tool for the questionnaire to be taken by the representatives from the ATS sample. The ATS representatives were emailed a link to the online survey. The survey technology allowed me to do content analysis and text analysis of the survey responses (Merriam, 2009). This analysis allowed me to code, filter, cross tabulate and organize the responses into a case study database in preparation for the final stage of the qualitative research study, the case study report (Yin, 2009).

The next and final section of this methodology chapter discusses the results of the pilot online survey conducted at a Protestant theological seminary in the northeast of the United States for this research study.

Pilot Study Results

On March 19, 2012, I conducted a pilot online survey with two respondents, the dean and president of a northeast theological seminary. The average response time for completing the questionnaire was approximately 25 minutes. The two respondents' answers were very helpful in assessing whether these questions would allow me to answer the three guiding research questions of this study. The following are the initial pilot survey questions:

1.  Has your theological school conducted an environmental scan(s) of the threats and opportunities impacting your racial and ethnic minority administrators, faculty, staff, and or students?

2. What have you identified as high priority issues of the changing environmental threats and opportunities of your racial and ethnic minority administrators, faculty, staff, and or students for your theological school?

3. Does your theological school presently have the resources to address, anticipate, respond to, and manage the environmental threats and opportunities effectively?

4. How is your theological school responding to present environmental threats and opportunities of your racial and ethnic minority administrators, faculty, staff, and or students?

5. How is your theological school preparing for the threats and opportunities in the changing external environment of racial and ethnic minority administrators, faculty, staff, and or students?

6. What is your position at the theological school?

7. For the purpose of this survey and the interview, please select all that applies (Permission to use your school name and position title in the study report).

8. What is the enrollment size of your school?

9. If selected, are you available for a 30 minute telephone interview?

10. What is your contact information?

The respondents who were chosen for a telephone interview were asked to clarify their responses to the survey questions.

The following is a summary of the responses by the dean and president of the northeast theological seminary and they are categorized according to the three guiding research questions for this study:

1. How many accredited ATS schools in the United States have conducted environmental scans of their institutions in order to identify threats and opportunities impacting their racial and ethnic minority administrators, faculty, staff, and students?

a. We pay attention to some of the realities faced by community members from racial/ethnic minorities. The Seminary has become attentive to issues related to the "criminal justice" system and the disproportionate imprisonment of persons of color. This "scanning" is also part of what our Anti-Racism Transformation Team does. But, we have not engaged in a "systematic collection of information" specifically focused on the threats and opportunities impacting racial and ethnic minority administrators, faculty, staff or students (dean of seminary).

2. Do the ATS schools in the United States have a shared understanding of high priority issues and views of the changing environmental threats and opportunities impacting their racial and ethnic minority administrators, faculty, staff, and students?

   a. The high priority issues include the following: 1. student debt-- all students but especially attentive to the fact that racial and ethnic minority students may tend to carry more debt given the lack of intergenerational assets

resulting from systemic racism;

2. Imprisonment and "criminal

justice" which requires

seminaries and churches to

respond for the sake of real

justice; 3. Students' knowledge

of their own peoples' history

and its impact on them,

congregations, etc. Through

our work with the ATS

Consultation on Race and

Ethnicity, we are now

assessing the culture and ethos

and how it must change in

order to welcome the voice,

perspective, concerns, gifts of

racial and ethnic members of the faculty/administration; 4. Student readiness for graduate theological education and the need for educational support-we are aware but need to work toward a comprehensive institutional response; 5. Racial and ethnic minority students may be bringing higher needs for psychological, emotional, spiritual support given the effect of systemic racism in the U.S.; and 6. Opportunity to support racial and ethnic minority students toward Ph.D.

study that could continue to expand and diversify the pool of faculty to teach in theological schools/universities (dean of seminary).

3. How are the ATS schools in the United States responding to and preparing for the threats and opportunities in the changing external environment of racial and ethnic minority administrators, faculty, staff, and students?

   a. One of our key resources is the institutional will and human commitment to respond to the threats and opportunities. I think we are growing the will and commitment. We are beginning to see what resources we need (financial support for professional therapy, for academic support services, scholarship aid, etc.). With a deep institutional commitment- we have an increasing number of colleagues who see and are prepared to act- the seminary continues to maintain a modest budget to this end (dean of seminary and president).

b. The clear identification of the Seminary as an anti-racist institution has drawn faculty and staff who have a similar commitment- the creation of an Anti-Racist Transformation Team has provided a forum to discuss and act on threats and opportunities- the commitment of the Board of Trustees has moved from implicit to explicit (president).

c. We are attending to student needs in process of curriculum revision, increasing the number of courses that address the history and present reality of racial and ethnic minority students, making sure that all courses are attentive to the hopes and concerns of these communities. We are assessing the culture and ethos so that it is genuinely open to all the voices/gifts/concerns of the whole community. We are appointing new faculty and staff who reflect the racial and ethnic diversity of the student body. We are now offering a Doctor of Ministry focused on Prisons, Public Policy and Transformative Justice. We are now offering a Certificate in Theological Studies in Spanish, and a similar program for Asian American persons in congregational leadership

(dean of seminary).

The two respondents gave me very helpful feedback for improving the survey instrument during my brief interviews with them for the purpose of clarifying their responses. The first suggestion given by the respondents was to expand on the purpose statement of the study in the introductory remarks of the survey. The second suggestion was to give the respondent the opportunity to identify their environmental scan as formal or informal in order to increase the number of responses. The third suggestion was to give the respondent more instructions for navigating through the survey.

The constructive feedback has been incorporated in the revised version of the survey instrument along with a shift from a focus on environmental scanning to one of the outcomes of environmental scanning, a strategic plan, for the research study. The dean of the seminary introduced the faculty and senior administrators to the concept of formal and informal environmental scanning process as part of the 2 year process of developing a strategic plan. The dean assisted me in identifying additional periodicals on environmental scanning used by her seminary that would be helpful. Environment scanning is relatively a new concept in theological strategic planning so very little is presently written, but I identified the most relevant periodicals in the literature review. In consultation with the dean after the implementation of the pilot survey, I decided the best way to answer the research questions would be to focus on one of the outcomes of the environmental scan, the strategic plan. In addition to the survey questions, I will also analyze the strategic plan documents provided by the the Protestant ATS accredited schools through their survey responses or their institutional websites. The respondents chosen for an interview were chosen for the purpose of clarifying their strategic plans and survey responses. The following are the revised survey questions:

1. Has your school developed and implemented a strategic plan in order to respond to the threats and opportunities impacting your racial and ethnic minority administrators, faculty, staff, and students and institutional climate?

2. What have you identified as high priority issues in the changing external environmental threats and opportunities impacting your racial and ethnic minority administrators, faculty, staff, and students and institutional climate?

3. How is your school responding to the present environmental threats and opportunities impacting your racial and ethnic minority administrators, faculty, staff, and students and institutional climate identified in your strategic plan?

4. How is your school preparing for future threats and opportunities in the changing external environment which

may impact your racial and ethnic minority administrators, faculty, staff, and students and institutional climate?

5. How has the strategic planning process impacted the institutional climate of your school?

6. Does your school presently have the resources to address, anticipate, respond to, and manage these environmental threats and opportunities effectively?

7. Can you provide a copy or website link of your most recent racial and ethnic strategic diversity plan for this research study? (If yes, please send strategic plan to email provided)?

8. What is the denominational affiliation of your school?

9. What is the enrollment size of your school?

10. If selected for additional questions about your strategic plan, are you available   for a 30 minute telephone interview?

11. For the purpose of this survey and an interview, please select all that applies (Permission to use your school name and position title in the study report).

12. What is your contact information?

The next chapter provides the conclusion for this report with a summary of the qualitative research study report, "An Environmental Scan of Racial and

Ethnic Minority Strategic Planning at U.S. Accredited Theological Schools."

# CHAPTER 4
## CONCLUSION

Summary

The Association of Theological Schools is a North American membership organization of more than 250 Protestant, Roman Catholic, and Orthodox graduate schools in the United States and Canada that grant post-baccalaureate professional and academic degrees. The Association of Theological Schools is the context for this qualitative research study report, "An Environmental Scan of Racial and Ethnic

Minority Strategic Planning at U.S. Accredited Theological Schools."

This qualitative research study conducted a case study of the strategic racial and ethnic minority plans being implemented at the accredited ATS schools in the United States that are affiliated with mainstream Protestant denominations and have begun to identify and respond to the opportunities and threats impacting racial and ethnic minority administrators, faculty, staff, and students and their institutional climates.

The goal of this qualitative research study is to provide the Association of Theological Schools with an assessment of the most recent strategic minority plans of these ATS accredited theological schools in the United States in order to assist the Association with fulfilling its diversity mission to assist their accredited schools with effectively identifying and responding to the changing ethnic and racial demographics taking place in the United States and as a result at its theological schools in order to ensure ATS accredited theological schools have continued relevance in theological education.

# CHAPTER FIVE
## References

Aguilar, F. (1967). *Scanning the business environment.* New York: MacMillan.

Aleshire, D. (2010). *The future has arrived: Changing theological education in a changed world.* Retrieved November 1, 2011 from http://www.ats.edu/Resources/PublicationsPresentations/Documents/BiennialMeetings/2010BiennialMeeting.aspx.

ATS (2002). Bulletin. Pittsburgh: The Association of Theological Schools.

ATS (2011). The association overview. Retrieved

November 1, 2011 from

http://www.ats.edu/about/Pages/default.aspx.

Brown, A., & Weiner, E. (1985). Supermanaging:

How to harness change for personal and

organizational success. New York: Mentor.

Cascante-Gomez, F.A. (2008). Advancing racial

ethnic diversity in theological education: A

model for reflection and action. *Theological

Education*, 43(2), 21-39.

Calian, C.S. (2002). The ideal seminary. Louisville:

Westminster John Knox Press.

Cheng, S. (2002). Racial differences in the effects of

significant others on students' educational

expectations. *Sociology of Education*, 75, 306.

Coates, J.F. (1985). Issues identification and

management: The state of the art of methods

and techniques (Research Project 2345-28).
Palo Alto: Electric Power Research Institute.

Cope, R.G. (1981). Environmental assessments for strategic planning. In N.L. Poulton, (ed.), *Evaluation of management and planning systems.* New Directions for Institutional Research, 31, 5-15. San Francisco: Jossey-Bass.

Crenshaw, K., Gotanda, N., Peller, G. & Thomas, K. (1995). *Critical race theory: The key writings that formed the movement.* New York: The New Press.

Dalrympie, M. (2009). Strategic planning in higher education: comparative perspectives in evaluation. LaVergne, TN: VDM Publishing House Ltd.

Darder, A., Baltodano, M. & Torres, R. (2003). *The critical pedagogy reader*. New York: RoutledgeFalmer.

Delgado, R. & Stefancic, J. (2001). *Critical race theory: An introduction*. New York: New York University Press.

Delgado, R. & Stefancic, J. (2000). *Critical race theory: The cutting edge*. Philadelphia: Temple University Press.

Fahey, L., King, W.R., & Narayanan, V.K. (1981). Environmental scanning and forecasting in strategic planning: The state of the art. *Long Range Planning*, 14(1), 32-39.

Foss, S. K. & Waters, W. (2007) Destination dissertation: A traveler's guide to a done dissertation. New York: Roman & Littlefield Publishers, Inc.

Frank, T.E. (2006). Polity, practice, and the mission of the United Methodist Church. Nashville: Abingdon Press.

Freire, P. (1998). *Pedagogy of freedom.* New York: Rowman & Littlefield Publishers, Inc.

Freire, P. (1993). *Pedagogy of the oppressed.* New York: The Continuum International Publishing Group Inc.

Hinchey, P.H. (2004). *Becoming a critical educator: Defining a classroom Identity, designing a critical pedagogy.* New York: Peter Lang.

Johnson, V. D. (2003). A comparison of European and African-based psychologies and their implications for African American college student development. *Journal of Black Studies, 33* (6), 820.

Kaufman, R., Herman, J., & Watters, K. (1996). Educational planning: strategic, tactical , and operational. Lancaster, PA: Technomic Publishing Company, Inc.

Keller, G. (1983). Academic strategy: The management revolution in American higher education. Baltimore, MD: Johns Hopkins University Press.

Kobrak, P. (1992). Black student retention in predominantly White regional universities: The politics of faculty involvement. *Journal of Negro Education, 61* (4), 509-519.

Kumashiro, K. (2004). Against common sense; *Teaching and learning toward social justice.* New York: RoutledgeFalmer.

Lonsway, F.A. (2002). Student diversity and the data. *Theological Education.*38(2), 51-62.

Mejido, M.J. (1998). U.S. Hispanics/latinos and the field of theological education. *Theological Education*. 34(2), 59-71.

Merriam, S.B. (2009). Qualitative research: A guide to design and implementation. San Francisco: Jossey-Boss.

Morrill, R.L. (2007). Strategic leadership: integrating strategy and leadership in colleges and universities. New York: Rowan & Littlefield Publishers, Inc.

Morrison, J.L. (1985). Establishing an environmental scanning process. In Davis, R.M. (Ed.) *Leadership and institutional renewal* (pp. 31-38). San Francisco: Jossey-Boss.

Morrison, J.L. (1986). Establishing an environmental scanning system to augment college and university planning. Planning for Higher

Education, 15(1), 7-22.

Morrison, J.L. (1992). Environmental scanning. In A.

Whitely, J.D. Porter, and R.H. Fenske (Eds.).

*A primer for new institutional researchers*

(pp. 86-99). Tallahassee, Florida: The

Association for Institutional Research.

Morrison, J.L. & Renfro. (1983). The scanning

process: Getting started. In Morrison, J.L.,

Renfro, W.L., & Boucher, W.I. *Applying*

*methods and techniques of future research*

(pp. 5-20), San Francisco: Jossey-Bass.

Pacala, L. (1998). The role of ATS in theological

education, 1980-1990. Atlanta: Scholars

Press.

Rowley, D.J., Lujan, H.D. & Dolence, M.G. (1997).

Strategic change in colleges and universities:

planning to survive and prosper. San Francisco: Jossey-Bass.

Rowley, D.J. & Sherman, H. (2004). Academic planning: The heart and soul of the academic strategic plan. New York: University Press of America, Inc.

Santrock, J. W. (2001). Educational psychology. St. Louis: Hill Higher Education.

Schmader, T., Major, B., & Gramzow, R. H. (2002, spring). How African-American college students protect their self-esteem. *The Journal of Blacks in Higher Education*, *35*,     116-118.

Schunk, D. H. (2004). Learning theories: An educational perspective (4th ed.). Upper Saddle River, NJ: Pearson Prentice Hall.

Shields, C.M (2007). Can case studies achieve the "Gold Standard"? Or when methodology meets politics. Paper presentation at the Annual Meeting of the American Education Research Association, Chicago,Illinois.

Speller, J.M. (2002). Increasing diversity in theological schools: A reflection. *Diversity in Education* (pp. 5-7). Pittsburgh: The Association of Theological Schools.

Stake, R.E., (2005). Qualitative case studies. In N.K. Denzin & Y.S. Lincoln (Eds.). *The Sage handbook of qualitative research.* (pp.443-466). Thomas Oaks, CA: Sage.

Suarez-Balcazar, Y., Orellana-Damacela, L., Portillo, N., Rowan, J. M., & Andrews-Guillen, C. (July/August 2003). Experiences of differential treatment among college students of color. *The Journal of Higher Education*, *74* (4), 430.

Tsui, L. (2003, summer). Reproducing social inequalities through higher education: Critical thinking as valued capital. *Journal of Negro Education*, *72* (3).

U.S. Census Bureau (2001). Census 2000 redistricting data. Washington: U.S. Department of Commerce.

Wong, P., Chienping Faith Lai, Nagasawa, R., & Lin, T. (1998). Asian Americans as a model minority: Self-perceptions and perceptions by other racial groups. *Sociological Perspectives*, *41* (1), 96-98.

Yin, R.K. (2009) Case Study Research: design and methods. Los Angeles: SAGE Publications, Inc.

# ABOUT THE AUTHOR

Dr. Jessica Davis is the president and senior government affairs advisor of the Faith & Public Policy Institute in Princeton, New Jersey and Washington, D.C. Dr. Davis is the host of The Moral Agenda, a weekly television broadcast educating the viewers on domestic and foreign policy seen on The WORD network reaching 85 million U.S. households and 200 countries. Dr. Davis is the senior pastor of St. Paul United Methodist Church in Mt. Holly, New Jersey. She is the first female pastor in the 127 year history of the church. Dr. Davis is the Doctor of Ministry faculty mentor for the Womanist Leadership in Ministry cohort at United Theological Seminary in Dayton, Ohio. Dr. Davis is a sought after consultant, lecturer, and preacher in both academic and faith communities.

Dr. Davis is a former Protestant seminary dean and Jesuit university dean. Dr. Davis is a member of the American Academy of Religion. She is a member of the Covenant Ecumenical Fellowship and Cathedral Assemblies, Inc. in Perth Amboy, New Jersey.

Dr. Davis served on the staff of the Boston Theological Institute (BTI), an ecumenical consortium of nine seminaries and graduate schools in the Greater Boston area, with the responsibility of developing ecumenical urban programming for the consortium. In her role, she traveled to Bangalore, India; Geneva, Switzerland; and Rome, Italy with BTI faculty, pastors, seminarians and staff to discuss ecumenism from a global perspective. During her visit to Rome, Pope John Paul II granted their travel group with a private audience at the Vatican. Pope John Paul II recognized and affirmed their commitment to ecumenism.

Dr. Davis earned the Doctor of Ministry from United Theological Seminary in Dayton, Ohio with a focus on social justice in Appalachian communities. She earned the Juris Doctor from Boston University School of Law, ranked as one of the top twenty law schools in the nation, after receiving the Master of Divinity from the School of Theology at Boston University in philosophical theology and social ethics. She is a candidate for the Doctor of Philosophy in Education at Southern Illinois University Carbondale.

**Dr. Davis is available for Strategic Planning, Diversity, and Enrollment consultation. To contact Dr. Davis, call Faith & Public Policy Institute Princeton at (609) 955-3547 or email Dr. Davis at president@faithpolicyinstitute.org.**

Proceeds from the purchase of this book supports the mission of the Faith & Public Policy Institute to educate the faith community on domestic and foreign policy to eradicate poverty. Thank you.